Masonic Roll of Fellow Crafts

Lodge__________________________________ No.__________

Enrollment Dates from _______________ to _______________

Bro.
JAMES F. HATCHER III, P.M.

Copyright © 2014
Bro. James F. Hatcher III, P.M.

All rights reserved.

ISBN-13: 978-1496018878
ISBN-10: 1496018877

Available from Amazon.com, CreateSpace.com, and other retail outlets

www.CreateSpace.com/4681538

Printed by CreateSpace, Charleston SC
An Amazon.com Company

MASONIC ROLL OF FELLOW CRAFTS

Date Enrolled	Name of Fellow Craft	Name of Worshipful Master	Name of Secretary

MASONIC ROLL OF FELLOW CRAFTS

Date Enrolled	Name of Fellow Craft	Name of Worshipful Master	Name of Secretary

MASONIC ROLL OF FELLOW CRAFTS

Date Enrolled	Name of Fellow Craft	Name of Worshipful Master	Name of Secretary

MASONIC ROLL OF FELLOW CRAFTS

Date Enrolled	Name of Fellow Craft	Name of Worshipful Master	Name of Secretary

MASONIC ROLL OF FELLOW CRAFTS

Date Enrolled	Name of Fellow Craft	Name of Worshipful Master	Name of Secretary

MASONIC ROLL OF FELLOW CRAFTS

Date Enrolled	Name of Fellow Craft	Name of Worshipful Master	Name of Secretary

MASONIC ROLL OF FELLOW CRAFTS

Date Enrolled	Name of Fellow Craft	Name of Worshipful Master	Name of Secretary

MASONIC ROLL OF FELLOW CRAFTS

Date Enrolled	Name of Fellow Craft	Name of Worshipful Master	Name of Secretary

MASONIC ROLL OF FELLOW CRAFTS

Date Enrolled	Name of Fellow Craft	Name of Worshipful Master	Name of Secretary

MASONIC ROLL OF FELLOW CRAFTS

Date Enrolled	Name of Fellow Craft	Name of Worshipful Master	Name of Secretary

MASONIC ROLL OF FELLOW CRAFTS

Date Enrolled	Name of Fellow Craft	Name of Worshipful Master	Name of Secretary

MASONIC ROLL OF FELLOW CRAFTS

Date Enrolled	Name of Fellow Craft	Name of Worshipful Master	Name of Secretary

MASONIC ROLL OF FELLOW CRAFTS

Date Enrolled	Name of Fellow Craft	Name of Worshipful Master	Name of Secretary

MASONIC ROLL OF FELLOW CRAFTS

Date Enrolled	Name of Fellow Craft	Name of Worshipful Master	Name of Secretary

MASONIC ROLL OF FELLOW CRAFTS

Date Enrolled	Name of Fellow Craft	Name of Worshipful Master	Name of Secretary

MASONIC ROLL OF FELLOW CRAFTS

Date Enrolled	Name of Fellow Craft	Name of Worshipful Master	Name of Secretary

MASONIC ROLL OF FELLOW CRAFTS

Date Enrolled	Name of Fellow Craft	Name of Worshipful Master	Name of Secretary

MASONIC ROLL OF FELLOW CRAFTS

Date Enrolled	Name of Fellow Craft	Name of Worshipful Master	Name of Secretary

MASONIC ROLL OF FELLOW CRAFTS

Date Enrolled	Name of Fellow Craft	Name of Worshipful Master	Name of Secretary

MASONIC ROLL OF FELLOW CRAFTS

Date Enrolled	Name of Fellow Craft	Name of Worshipful Master	Name of Secretary

MASONIC ROLL OF FELLOW CRAFTS

Date Enrolled	Name of Fellow Craft	Name of Worshipful Master	Name of Secretary

MASONIC ROLL OF FELLOW CRAFTS

Date Enrolled	Name of Fellow Craft	Name of Worshipful Master	Name of Secretary

MASONIC ROLL OF FELLOW CRAFTS

Date Enrolled	Name of Fellow Craft	Name of Worshipful Master	Name of Secretary

MASONIC ROLL OF FELLOW CRAFTS

Date Enrolled	Name of Fellow Craft	Name of Worshipful Master	Name of Secretary

MASONIC ROLL OF FELLOW CRAFTS

Date Enrolled	Name of Fellow Craft	Name of Worshipful Master	Name of Secretary

MASONIC ROLL OF FELLOW CRAFTS

Date Enrolled	Name of Fellow Craft	Name of Worshipful Master	Name of Secretary

MASONIC ROLL OF FELLOW CRAFTS

Date Enrolled	Name of Fellow Craft	Name of Worshipful Master	Name of Secretary

MASONIC ROLL OF FELLOW CRAFTS

Date Enrolled	Name of Fellow Craft	Name of Worshipful Master	Name of Secretary

MASONIC ROLL OF FELLOW CRAFTS

Date Enrolled	Name of Fellow Craft	Name of Worshipful Master	Name of Secretary

MASONIC ROLL OF FELLOW CRAFTS

Date Enrolled	Name of Fellow Craft	Name of Worshipful Master	Name of Secretary

MASONIC ROLL OF FELLOW CRAFTS

Date Enrolled	Name of Fellow Craft	Name of Worshipful Master	Name of Secretary

MASONIC ROLL OF FELLOW CRAFTS

Date Enrolled	Name of Fellow Craft	Name of Worshipful Master	Name of Secretary

MASONIC ROLL OF FELLOW CRAFTS

Date Enrolled	Name of Fellow Craft	Name of Worshipful Master	Name of Secretary

MASONIC ROLL OF FELLOW CRAFTS

Date Enrolled	Name of Fellow Craft	Name of Worshipful Master	Name of Secretary

MASONIC ROLL OF FELLOW CRAFTS

Date Enrolled	Name of Fellow Craft	Name of Worshipful Master	Name of Secretary

MASONIC ROLL OF FELLOW CRAFTS

Date Enrolled	Name of Fellow Craft	Name of Worshipful Master	Name of Secretary

MASONIC ROLL OF FELLOW CRAFTS

Date Enrolled	Name of Fellow Craft	Name of Worshipful Master	Name of Secretary

MASONIC ROLL OF FELLOW CRAFTS

Date Enrolled	Name of Fellow Craft	Name of Worshipful Master	Name of Secretary

MASONIC ROLL OF FELLOW CRAFTS

Date Enrolled	Name of Fellow Craft	Name of Worshipful Master	Name of Secretary

MASONIC ROLL OF FELLOW CRAFTS

Date Enrolled	Name of Fellow Craft	Name of Worshipful Master	Name of Secretary

MASONIC ROLL OF FELLOW CRAFTS

Date Enrolled	Name of Fellow Craft	Name of Worshipful Master	Name of Secretary

MASONIC ROLL OF FELLOW CRAFTS

Date Enrolled	Name of Fellow Craft	Name of Worshipful Master	Name of Secretary

MASONIC ROLL OF FELLOW CRAFTS

Date Enrolled	Name of Fellow Craft	Name of Worshipful Master	Name of Secretary

MASONIC ROLL OF FELLOW CRAFTS

Date Enrolled	Name of Fellow Craft	Name of Worshipful Master	Name of Secretary

MASONIC ROLL OF FELLOW CRAFTS

Date Enrolled	Name of Fellow Craft	Name of Worshipful Master	Name of Secretary

MASONIC ROLL OF FELLOW CRAFTS

Date Enrolled	Name of Fellow Craft	Name of Worshipful Master	Name of Secretary

MASONIC ROLL OF FELLOW CRAFTS

Date Enrolled	Name of Fellow Craft	Name of Worshipful Master	Name of Secretary

MASONIC ROLL OF FELLOW CRAFTS

Date Enrolled	Name of Fellow Craft	Name of Worshipful Master	Name of Secretary

MASONIC ROLL OF FELLOW CRAFTS

Date Enrolled	Name of Fellow Craft	Name of Worshipful Master	Name of Secretary

MASONIC ROLL OF FELLOW CRAFTS

Date Enrolled	Name of Fellow Craft	Name of Worshipful Master	Name of Secretary

MASONIC ROLL OF FELLOW CRAFTS

Date Enrolled	Name of Fellow Craft	Name of Worshipful Master	Name of Secretary

MASONIC ROLL OF FELLOW CRAFTS

Date Enrolled	Name of Fellow Craft	Name of Worshipful Master	Name of Secretary

MASONIC ROLL OF FELLOW CRAFTS

Date Enrolled	Name of Fellow Craft	Name of Worshipful Master	Name of Secretary

MASONIC ROLL OF FELLOW CRAFTS

Date Enrolled	Name of Fellow Craft	Name of Worshipful Master	Name of Secretary

MASONIC ROLL OF FELLOW CRAFTS

Date Enrolled	Name of Fellow Craft	Name of Worshipful Master	Name of Secretary

MASONIC ROLL OF FELLOW CRAFTS

Date Enrolled	Name of Fellow Craft	Name of Worshipful Master	Name of Secretary

MASONIC ROLL OF FELLOW CRAFTS

Date Enrolled	Name of Fellow Craft	Name of Worshipful Master	Name of Secretary

MASONIC ROLL OF FELLOW CRAFTS

Date Enrolled	Name of Fellow Craft	Name of Worshipful Master	Name of Secretary

MASONIC ROLL OF FELLOW CRAFTS

Date Enrolled	Name of Fellow Craft	Name of Worshipful Master	Name of Secretary

MASONIC ROLL OF FELLOW CRAFTS

Date Enrolled	Name of Fellow Craft	Name of Worshipful Master	Name of Secretary

MASONIC ROLL OF FELLOW CRAFTS

Date Enrolled	Name of Fellow Craft	Name of Worshipful Master	Name of Secretary

MASONIC ROLL OF FELLOW CRAFTS

Date Enrolled	Name of Fellow Craft	Name of Worshipful Master	Name of Secretary

MASONIC ROLL OF FELLOW CRAFTS

Date Enrolled	Name of Fellow Craft	Name of Worshipful Master	Name of Secretary

MASONIC ROLL OF FELLOW CRAFTS

Date Enrolled	Name of Fellow Craft	Name of Worshipful Master	Name of Secretary

MASONIC ROLL OF FELLOW CRAFTS

Date Enrolled	Name of Fellow Craft	Name of Worshipful Master	Name of Secretary

MASONIC ROLL OF FELLOW CRAFTS

Date Enrolled	Name of Fellow Craft	Name of Worshipful Master	Name of Secretary

MASONIC ROLL OF FELLOW CRAFTS

Date Enrolled	Name of Fellow Craft	Name of Worshipful Master	Name of Secretary

MASONIC ROLL OF FELLOW CRAFTS

Date Enrolled	Name of Fellow Craft	Name of Worshipful Master	Name of Secretary

MASONIC ROLL OF FELLOW CRAFTS

Date Enrolled	Name of Fellow Craft	Name of Worshipful Master	Name of Secretary

MASONIC ROLL OF FELLOW CRAFTS

Date Enrolled	Name of Fellow Craft	Name of Worshipful Master	Name of Secretary

MASONIC ROLL OF FELLOW CRAFTS

Date Enrolled	Name of Fellow Craft	Name of Worshipful Master	Name of Secretary

MASONIC ROLL OF FELLOW CRAFTS

Date Enrolled	Name of Fellow Craft	Name of Worshipful Master	Name of Secretary

MASONIC ROLL OF FELLOW CRAFTS

Date Enrolled	Name of Fellow Craft	Name of Worshipful Master	Name of Secretary

MASONIC ROLL OF FELLOW CRAFTS

Date Enrolled	Name of Fellow Craft	Name of Worshipful Master	Name of Secretary

MASONIC ROLL OF FELLOW CRAFTS

Date Enrolled	Name of Fellow Craft	Name of Worshipful Master	Name of Secretary

MASONIC ROLL OF FELLOW CRAFTS

Date Enrolled	Name of Fellow Craft	Name of Worshipful Master	Name of Secretary

MASONIC ROLL OF FELLOW CRAFTS

Date Enrolled	Name of Fellow Craft	Name of Worshipful Master	Name of Secretary

MASONIC ROLL OF FELLOW CRAFTS

Date Enrolled	Name of Fellow Craft	Name of Worshipful Master	Name of Secretary

MASONIC ROLL OF FELLOW CRAFTS

Date Enrolled	Name of Fellow Craft	Name of Worshipful Master	Name of Secretary

MASONIC ROLL OF FELLOW CRAFTS

Date Enrolled	Name of Fellow Craft	Name of Worshipful Master	Name of Secretary

MASONIC ROLL OF FELLOW CRAFTS

Date Enrolled	Name of Fellow Craft	Name of Worshipful Master	Name of Secretary

MASONIC ROLL OF FELLOW CRAFTS

Date Enrolled	Name of Fellow Craft	Name of Worshipful Master	Name of Secretary

MASONIC ROLL OF FELLOW CRAFTS

Date Enrolled	Name of Fellow Craft	Name of Worshipful Master	Name of Secretary

MASONIC ROLL OF FELLOW CRAFTS

Date Enrolled	Name of Fellow Craft	Name of Worshipful Master	Name of Secretary

MASONIC ROLL OF FELLOW CRAFTS

Date Enrolled	Name of Fellow Craft	Name of Worshipful Master	Name of Secretary

MASONIC ROLL OF FELLOW CRAFTS

Date Enrolled	Name of Fellow Craft	Name of Worshipful Master	Name of Secretary

MASONIC ROLL OF FELLOW CRAFTS

Date Enrolled	Name of Fellow Craft	Name of Worshipful Master	Name of Secretary

MASONIC ROLL OF FELLOW CRAFTS

Date Enrolled	Name of Fellow Craft	Name of Worshipful Master	Name of Secretary

MASONIC ROLL OF FELLOW CRAFTS

Date Enrolled	Name of Fellow Craft	Name of Worshipful Master	Name of Secretary

MASONIC ROLL OF FELLOW CRAFTS

Date Enrolled	Name of Fellow Craft	Name of Worshipful Master	Name of Secretary

MASONIC ROLL OF FELLOW CRAFTS

Date Enrolled	Name of Fellow Craft	Name of Worshipful Master	Name of Secretary

MASONIC ROLL OF FELLOW CRAFTS

Date Enrolled	Name of Fellow Craft	Name of Worshipful Master	Name of Secretary

MASONIC ROLL OF FELLOW CRAFTS

Date Enrolled	Name of Fellow Craft	Name of Worshipful Master	Name of Secretary

MASONIC ROLL OF FELLOW CRAFTS

Date Enrolled	Name of Fellow Craft	Name of Worshipful Master	Name of Secretary

MASONIC ROLL OF FELLOW CRAFTS

Date Enrolled	Name of Fellow Craft	Name of Worshipful Master	Name of Secretary

MASONIC ROLL OF FELLOW CRAFTS

Date Enrolled	Name of Fellow Craft	Name of Worshipful Master	Name of Secretary

MASONIC ROLL OF FELLOW CRAFTS

Date Enrolled	Name of Fellow Craft	Name of Worshipful Master	Name of Secretary

MASONIC ROLL OF FELLOW CRAFTS

Date Enrolled	Name of Fellow Craft	Name of Worshipful Master	Name of Secretary

MASONIC ROLL OF FELLOW CRAFTS

Date Enrolled	Name of Fellow Craft	Name of Worshipful Master	Name of Secretary

MASONIC ROLL OF FELLOW CRAFTS

Date Enrolled	Name of Fellow Craft	Name of Worshipful Master	Name of Secretary

MASONIC ROLL OF FELLOW CRAFTS

Date Enrolled	Name of Fellow Craft	Name of Worshipful Master	Name of Secretary

MASONIC ROLL OF FELLOW CRAFTS

Date Enrolled	Name of Fellow Craft	Name of Worshipful Master	Name of Secretary

MASONIC ROLL OF FELLOW CRAFTS

Date Enrolled	Name of Fellow Craft	Name of Worshipful Master	Name of Secretary

MASONIC ROLL OF FELLOW CRAFTS

Date Enrolled	Name of Fellow Craft	Name of Worshipful Master	Name of Secretary

MASONIC ROLL OF FELLOW CRAFTS

Date Enrolled	Name of Fellow Craft	Name of Worshipful Master	Name of Secretary

MASONIC ROLL OF FELLOW CRAFTS

Date Enrolled	Name of Fellow Craft	Name of Worshipful Master	Name of Secretary

MASONIC ROLL OF FELLOW CRAFTS

Date Enrolled	Name of Fellow Craft	Name of Worshipful Master	Name of Secretary

MASONIC ROLL OF FELLOW CRAFTS

Date Enrolled	Name of Fellow Craft	Name of Worshipful Master	Name of Secretary

MASONIC ROLL OF FELLOW CRAFTS

Date Enrolled	Name of Fellow Craft	Name of Worshipful Master	Name of Secretary

ABOUT THE AUTHOR

Bro. James Frank Hatcher III, better known as "Chip," is a Master Mason and Past Worshipful Master of Rockford Masonic Lodge No. 469, Free and Accepted Masons of Tennessee, in Rockford, Tennessee ~ a small, quiet hamlet in the foothills of the Great Smoky Mountains in Eastern Tennessee. He lives with his wife, three children, three dogs, six cats, two hermit crabs, and nearby to many, many wonderful friends, whom he later found to be his Brothers in many, many different situations.

He is also the Author of the following books in the series,
Tools for the 21st Century Freemason:

Vol. 1
Worshipful Master's Guidebook, or the "Book of Joe"
www.createspace.com/4523383

Vol. 2
Lodge Officer's Handbook
www.createspace.com/4527286

Vol. 3
King Solomon's Passport
www.createspace.com/4531237

Vol. 4
Masonic Roll of Fellow Crafts
www.createspace.com/4681538

SO·MOTE·IT·BE

www.ingramcontent.com/pod-product-compliance
Lightning Source LLC
Chambersburg PA
CBHW080418290526
45791CB00008BA/2327
* 9 7 8 1 4 9 6 0 1 8 8 7 8 *